My World Minibeasts

	Page	CD track Vocal	backing
INTRODUCTION	3	–	
LYRICS & TEACHER'S NOTES	4	–	
THE SONGS			
If I Were A Minibeast	17	1	14
What A Beast!	20	2	15
Joey*	22	3	16
Follow The Silver Trail*	24	4	17
Hey, Mister Bee	26	5	18
Squirm	29	6	19
We're Strong Ants*	32	7	20
Pitter Patter Caterpillar	34	8	21
Please Don't Squish Me!	36	9	22
Out In The Garden	38	10	23
Spider Spins*	40	11	24
A B-U-G	42	12	25
Five Bluebottles* (Bonus track)	44	13	26

* Especially suitable for early years

© 2006 Out of the Ark Music

Introduction

The *My World* series of books is a brand new collection of topic-based songbooks. Each includes twelve easy-to-learn and catchy songs by some of Britain's most popular children's songwriters. The accompanying CD features all songs sung by children along with professionally produced backing tracks.

Developed specifically for pre-school and reception aged children, we feel that the music and topics covered will also be particularly appropriate for use with children up to the age of around seven. The songs can be used to supplement the 'creative' requirements of the foundation stage, as well as contributing to many other areas of the curriculum. Each lyric page contains helpful teacher's notes to expand and develop the subject content of the songs.

In addition to the teaching ideas given with each song, we suggest adding some simple percussion using instruments available in the classroom, and perhaps some homemade ones. It's important that children relate to music as something that they can become actively involved with and enjoy. Using percussion and easy clapping rhythms gives everyone a chance to really join in.

If I Were A Minibeast

Words and Music by Mark and Helen Johnson

1. If I were a minibeast,
   I wonder what I'd choose to be?
   A spider in a web?
   Or a cricket in a hedge?
   Maybe, ... let me see.

2. If I were a minibeast,
   I wonder what I'd choose to be?
   A ladybird with spots?
   Or a centipede with lots of legs?

   CHORUS *Would I like to jump?*
   Would I like to swim?
   Would I rather crawl, or fly with wings?
   These are just a few of the many things
   To choose between.

   Would I like to live under rocks or stones?
   In the sky above, or the earth below?
   Would it suit me best to live underneath the ground?

   Repeat song

Get the children to use their imagination and create some new and crazy minibeasts, perhaps ladybirds with stripes or spiders with fins. They could draw these or even build them to create a whole army of wacky minibeasts.

What A Beast!
Words and Music by Sha Armstrong

1. Hairy scary spider,
   Around me every day,
   Hairy scary spider,
   There's one thing I must say …

   CHORUS   *What a beast, what a beast,*
                           What a beast you are.
                           What a beast, what a fine minibeast you are.
                           What a beast, what a beast,
                           What a beast you are, Minibeast!

2. Wiggly, wriggly worm,
   Around me every day,
   Wiggly, wriggly worm,
   There's one thing I must say

   CHORUS

3. Slippery, slimy slug,
   Around me every day,
   Slippery, slimy slug,
   There's one thing I must say …

   CHORUS

4. Creepy, crawly beetle,
   Around me every day,
   Creepy, crawly beetle,
   There's one thing I must say …

   CHORUS x 2

- Move around the room like the creatures in each verse. You can add new verses of your own too.

- Talk about the fact that minibeasts are 'around us every day'. Can the children name some places they like to live?

Joey

Words and Music by Ali McClure

1. Joey is a frog and he goes
   Jump, jump, jump,
   Jump, jump, jump,
   Jump, jump, jump.
   Joey is a frog and he goes
   Jump, jump, jump,
   Jump, jump, jump, jump, jump.

2. When Joey was a tadpole he went
   Swim, swim, swim,
   Swim, swim, swim,
   Swim, swim, swim.
   When Joey was a tadpole he went
   Swim, swim, swim,
   Swim, swim, swim, swim, swim.

3. When Joey was in frogspawn he went
   Wobble, wobble, wobble,
   Wobble, wobble, wobble,
   Wobble, wobble, wobble.
   When Joey was in frogspawn he went
   Wobble, wobble, wobble,
   Wobble, wobble, wobble, wobble, wobble.

4. BUT, Joey is a frog and he goes
   Jump, jump, jump,
   Jump, jump, jump,
   Jump, jump, jump.
   Joey is a frog and he goes
   Jump, jump, jump,
   Jump, jump, jump, jump, jump.

- This is a great song for actions. They are pretty obvious and children especially love the 'wobbling' verse!

- Talk about the life cycle of a frog. If it's the right time of year you could collect some frogspawn and watch it develop into tadpoles. Don't forget to put it back when the tadpoles have grown.

- You can develop your discussions further to include talking about the passage of time and how humans change and grow over time too.

Follow The Silver Trail

Words and Music by Niki Davies

1. Follow, follow the silver trail,
   Where are you, Mister Snail?
   Are you under that leaf? No, no!
   It's only a beetle saying, "Hello".

2. Follow, follow the silver trail,
   Where are you, Mister Snail?
   Are you under that stone? No, no!
   It's only a centipede saying, "Hello".

3. Follow, follow the silver trail,
   Where are you, Mister Snail?
   Are you under that log? No, no!
   It's only an earwig saying, "Hello".

4. Follow, follow the silver trail,
   Where are you, Mister Snail?
   Are you where the strawberries grow?
   Yes, it's Mister Snail saying, "Hello".

- Make a snail 'house'. Use a transparent container and pierce this with a few air holes. Put some wet leaves in and add the snails that you've collected. Snails do not like hot and dry conditions, they prefer a moist, humid habitat which is not too bright. Make sure the container is kept moist. You'll be able to watch the snails and observe how they move and eat.

  After a few days put the snails back into their natural habitat. It's good to do this with the children so they learn the importance of returning creatures back where they came from.

Hey, Mister Bee

Words and Music by Mark and Helen Johnson

1. Hey, Mister Bee
    Can you see
    All the flowers around today?
    Hey, Mister Bee
    I can see
    There are lots to be found today.

    CHORUS   *When you've chosen a place,*
    Go dance in a figure of eight,
    To show everyone,
    Where to come
    For the pollen today.

Repeat song twice

After last chorus:
To show ev'ryone,
Where to come
For the pollen today.
So tell everyone
We'll have fun
Making honey today!

- It's true that honeybees have a special dance they perform once they have discovered a source of nectar. It consists of a circle dance and a tail wagging dance, that accurately tell other bees the angle from the sun and the distance to the nectar – clever stuff!

- Talk about why bees collect nectar and what they make from it. Talk about their hives and that there are drones, worker bees and a Queen Bee in each colony. Ask the children if they know why bees have a stinger. Have any of the children ever been stung by a bee? How did it feel?

Squirm

Words and Music by Ann Beresford

I have a little friend who's not a bit like me,
He's long and thin and squidgy and he's – wrinkly.
He hasn't any fingers, he hasn't any toes,
I don't think he's got any eyes or mouth or nose.
He hasn't got a front and he hasn't got a back,
He hasn't any teeth to go snap, snap, snap.
He doesn't make a buzzy noise or even just a cheep,
But he's very good at making earth down in the compost heap.

Have you guessed who my friend is yet?
I think I'll call him "Squirm",
'Cos he wriggles and he squiggles through the ground,
He's a worm!!!

- Earthworms play a vital role in helping to fertilise our soil – making it good to grow plants and food. If you have an area of garden at the school, why not go out and see if the children can spot any worms in the soil?

- Get the children to plant a few seeds in some soil and watch them grow into flowers over the next few weeks – it's a nice way to decorate the classroom.

- Have a table-top wormery to see how worms move the soil around etc.

We're Strong Ants

Words and Music by Niki Davies

1. We're strong ants, strong ants,
   We carry the food as we march along.
   We're strong ants, strong ants,
   Hup, two, three, four, strong ants.

2. We're buzzing bees, buzzing bees,
   We're making honey all day long.
   We're buzzing bees, buzzing bees,
   Buzz, buzz, buzz, buzz, buzzing bees.

3. We're butterflies, butterflies,
   We carry pollen from flower to flower.
   We're butterflies, butterflies,
   Flitter, flutter butterflies.

4. We're slimy worms, slimy worms,
   We tunnel all day inside the ground.
   We're slimy worms, slimy worms,
   Wriggly, squiggly slimy worms.

- The children can develop some good actions for this song.

- Talk about the important jobs that all the creatures in this song do. Talk about the shape of each of the creatures and how the way they are made helps them do their jobs, (a bee wouldn't be much use without it's wings and a worm couldn't slide through soil if it were spiky).

- Gather together some percussion instruments to help accompany this song. Ask the children to choose which sounds they think suit each verse (ie drum/ants; kazoo/bees; tambourines/butterflies; glissandos on glock/worm) and get them to play along as they sing the song.

Pitter Patter Caterpillar

Words and Music by Sha Armstrong

1. Pitter patter caterpillar crawling in the rain,
   Better get a move on now or you'll get wet again.
   Find a leaf to hide behind,
   Take a bite and you'll be fine,
   Pitter patter caterpillar, crawling in the rain.

2. Pitter patter caterpillar crawling in the rain,
   Better get a move on now or you'll get wet again.
   Find a flower to shelter you,
   Take a rest, you'll feel brand new,
   Pitter patter caterpillar, crawling in the rain.

3. Pitter patter caterpillar, crawling in the rain,
   Better get a move on now or you'll get wet again.
   Find a place for your cocoon,
   A butterfly you will be soon,
   Pitter patter caterpillar, crawling in the rain.

- Talk about different weather conditions with the children. How do they think the caterpillar will behave on a sunny day compared to a rainy one? Will it hide behind the leaves or bask in the sun on top of them?

- Ask the children to have a good look around their gardens to see if they can find any leaves that may have been eaten by caterpillars. What do they look like?

- Talk about the life cycle of caterpillars through to chrysalis/cocoon, then butterflies/moths. Here are a few facts you might want to include:

  * they eat leaves voraciously and grow rapidly
  * they shed their skins four or five times before making their cocoon
  * they do not have very good eyesight or senses and rely on their antennae to help locate food

Please Don't Squish Me!

Words and Music by Mark and Helen Johnson

You may think that I'm scary,
Or say I'm only small.
Perhaps you think that I'm no good for anything at all.
But actually it's clever
How I've been put together,
And if you get to know me you'll discover that I'm cool!

CHORUS
(So) Please don't squish me,
Please don't squash me!
Put me back exactly where you got me.
Please don't poke me,
Please don't prod me!
Let me be a happy minibeast.

You may think that I'm scary,
Or say I'm only small.
Perhaps you think that I'm no good for anything at all.
But actually it's clever
How I've been put together,
And if you get to know me you'll discover that I'm cool!

CHORUS x 2

Let me be a happy minibeast.

Ask the children to talk about how they feel when someone is unkind to them. How do they feel when someone is kind to them? Talk about the ways in which we can do more to help others around us – both animals and humans.

Out In The Garden

Words and Music by Ann Beresford

1. Out in the garden, underneath the stones,
   You'll find minibeasts who don't have bones,
   Earthworms and woodlice, centipedes and ants.
   Don't go sitting down on them – you'll get them in your pants.

2. Out in the garden, round the flowerpots,
   You'll find minibeasts with stripes or spots,
   Caterpillars, spiders, ladybirds and ants.
   Don't go sitting down on them – you'll get them in your pants.

3. Out in the garden, underneath a pail,
   You'll find minibeasts like slugs and snails,
   Beetles and earwigs, millipedes and ants.
   Don't go sitting down on them – you'll get them in your pants.

4. Out in the garden, resting on the leaves,
   You'll find minibeasts like wasps and bees,
   Butterflies and greenflies, dragonflies and ants.
   Don't go sitting down on them – you'll get them in your pants.

5. Out in the garden, by the compost heap,
   You'll find minibeasts that jump and leap,
   Crickets and spit bugs, grasshoppers and ants.
   Don't go sitting down on them – you'll get them in your pants.

Get the children to go out into their gardens – or the school one, if you have one – and see how many minibeasts they can find. Get them to count how many different things they see. What did they find the most of; what were the biggest and smallest; how many places did they find them in?

Spider Spins

Words and Music by Niki Davies

1. Spider spins at *one* o'clock,
   Busy, busy legs, she doesn't stop.
   Spinning, spinning silver threads,
   Busy, busy spider, make your web.

2. Spider spins at *two* o'clock,
   Busy, busy legs, she doesn't stop.
   Spinning, spinning silver threads,
   Busy, busy spider, make your web.

3. Spider spins at *three* o'clock,
   Busy, busy legs, she doesn't stop.
   Spinning, spinning silver threads,
   Busy, busy spider, make your web.

4. Spider spins at *four* o'clock,
   Busy, busy legs, she doesn't stop.
   Spinning, spinning silver threads,
   Busy, busy spider, make your web.

5. Spider spins at *five* o'clock,
   Busy, busy legs, she doesn't stop.
   Spinning, spinning silver threads,
   Busy, busy spider, make your web.

- Make a special piece of artwork to go with this song. You'll need a black piece of paper, some glue, some silver glitter and a silver pen. Write the numbers 1-12 in a circle around the edge of the paper (like a clock), then with the glue connect all the numbers together, going across the page and also from one number to the next to create a web. They can then add more web-like links between the lines already created. Sprinkle on the glitter and you have the spider's 'clock' web. The children can draw a spider on the web and perhaps a fly for it to catch!

- Talk about why spiders spin webs. What do they trap in them and why?

- Talk about how useful spiders are for us.

A B-U-G

Words and Music by Sha Armstrong

CHORUS *A B-U-G, a B-U-G,*
Everywhere I look I see a B-U-G.

1. They live under the carpet,
   They live under the stair,
   They live inside the cupboard
   Crawling everywhere.

   CHORUS

2. They hide down in the cellar,
   They hide under the ground,
   They hide in the dark corners,
   Crawling all around.

   CHORUS

3. They play out in the garden,
   They play under the swing,
   They play round by the dustbin,
   Crawling on everything.

   A B-U-G, a B-U-G,
   Everywhere I look I see a B-U-G.
   Everywhere I look I see a B-U-G!

What are the children's ideas of a 'bug'? Do they imagine real bugs (eg ants, beetles, spiders, centipedes, etc) or cartoon-type 'bugs'?

Create some imaginary bugs using cotton wool, pipe cleaners, string, cardboard – anything you have to hand – and then build a model 3D room or house to reflect the song. The children can place their bugs amongst the cupboards, corners and carpet of the model.

Five Bluebottles
(Bonus track)
Traditional. Adapted by Mark and Helen Johnson

1. Five bluebottles
   Sitting on the wall,
   Five bluebottles
   Sitting on the wall,
   And if one bluebottle
   Should accidentally fall ....*(Buzz!)*
   There'll be **four** bluebottles, sitting on the wall…

2. Four bluebottles …

3. Three bluebottles …

4. Two Bluebottles …

5. One bluebottle
   Sitting on the wall,
   One bluebottle
   Sitting on the wall,
   And if that bluebottle
   Should accidentally fall ....*(Buzz!)*
   There'll be **no** bluebottles, sitting on the wall*…

*Please note: no flies were harmed during the making of this song!

Just a bit of fun to end this collection – we hope you enjoy it!

If I Were A Minibeast

Words and Music by
Mark and Helen Johnson

Country shuffle ♩ = 120

1. If I were a mini-beast, I wonder what I'd choose to be, a spider in a web? Or a
2. If I were a mini-beast, I wonder what I'd choose to be, a lady-bird with spots? Or a

© 2006 Out of the Ark Music, Surrey KT12 4RQ

1.
2.
Ab7
Ebmaj7
cric - ket in a hedge? May - be, let me see.
cen - ti - pede with lots of legs?
Bb Bb7 Ab2/C Bb7/D
Eb
Eb Db2/F Eb7/G
Would I
Ab Ab/Eb Ab Bb7 Eb Eb/D
like to jump? Would I like to swim? Would I ra - ther crawl or
Cm7 Eb/Bb Bbsus4 Fm7 Fm7/Eb Bb7 Cm7 Bb7/D
fly with wings? These are just a few of the ma - ny things to

choose be - tween. Would I like to live un - der rocks or stones? In the sky a - bove, or the earth be - low? Would it suit me best to live un - der neath the ground?

To Coda ⊕ *D.S. al Coda* ⊕ **CODA**

What A Beast!

Words and Music by
Sha Armstrong

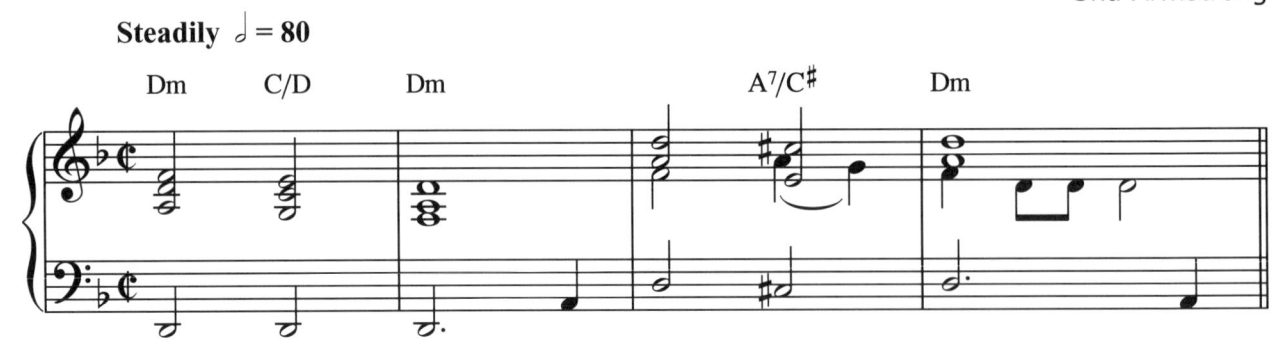

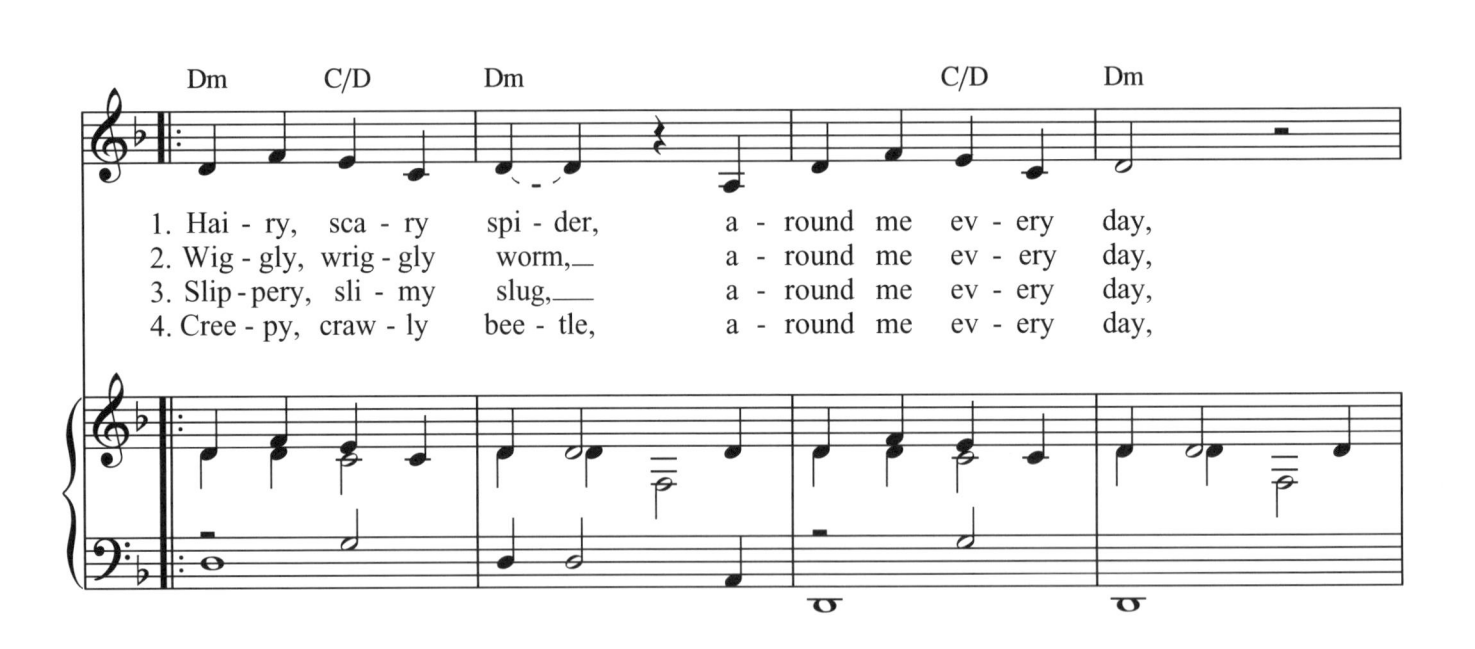

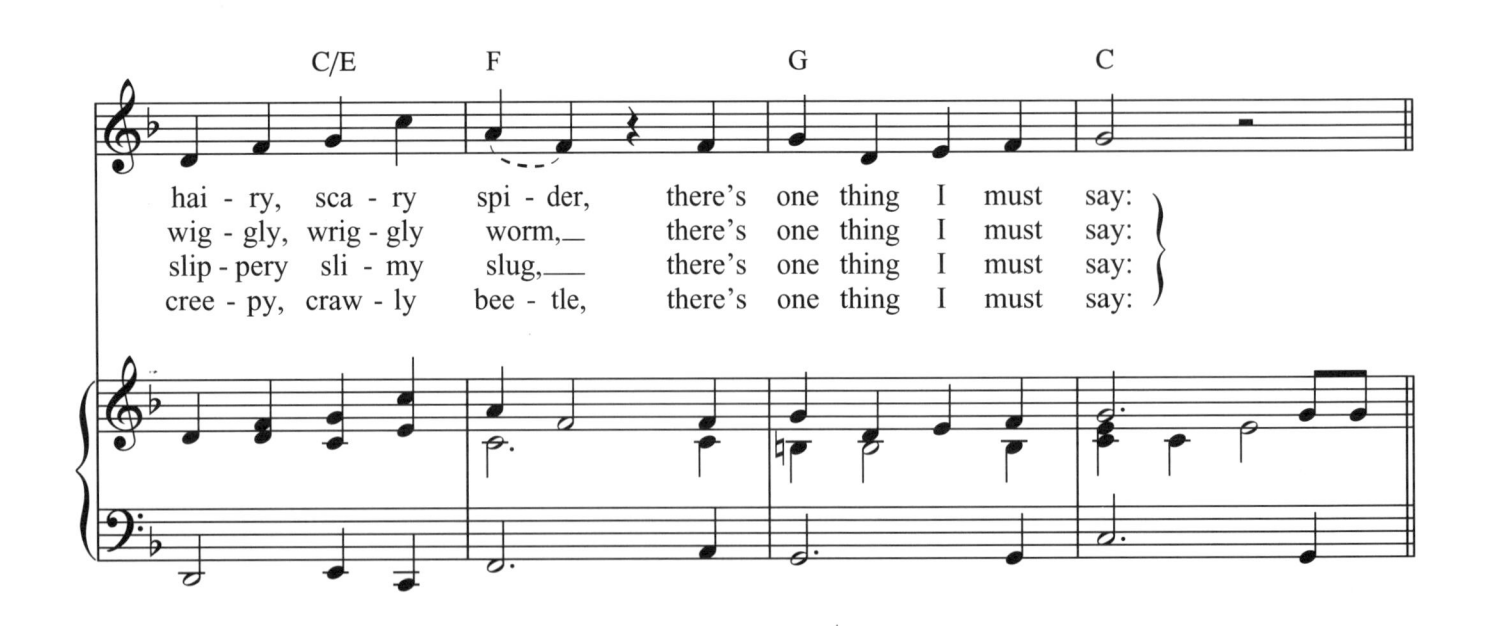

Steadily ♩ = 80

1. Hai - ry, sca - ry spi - der, a - round me ev - ery day,
2. Wig - gly, wrig - gly worm, a - round me ev - ery day,
3. Slip - pery, sli - my slug, a - round me ev - ery day,
4. Cree - py, craw - ly bee - tle, a - round me ev - ery day,

hai - ry, sca - ry spi - der, there's one thing I must say:
wig - gly, wrig - gly worm, there's one thing I must say:
slip - pery sli - my slug, there's one thing I must say:
cree - py, craw - ly bee - tle, there's one thing I must say:

© 2006 Out of the Ark Music, Surrey KT12 4RQ

What a beast, what a beast what a beast you are, what a beast, what a fine mini-beast you are, what a beast, what a beast what a beast you are,

mi-ni-beast!

-beast! What a mi-ni-beast!

Joey

Words and Music by
Ali McClure

Light 'n' croaky ♩ = 135

(A little slower for v.2 +3)

1. Jo-ey is a frog and he goes jump, jump, jump, jump, jump, jump,
(2.) Jo-ey was a tad-pole he went swim, swim, swim, swim, swim, swim,
(3.) Jo-ey was in frog-spawn he went wob-ble, wob-ble, wob-ble, wob-ble, wob-ble, wob-ble,
(4.) Jo-ey is a frog and he goes jump, jump, jump, jump, jump, jump,

© 2006 Out of the Ark Music, Surrey KT12 4RQ

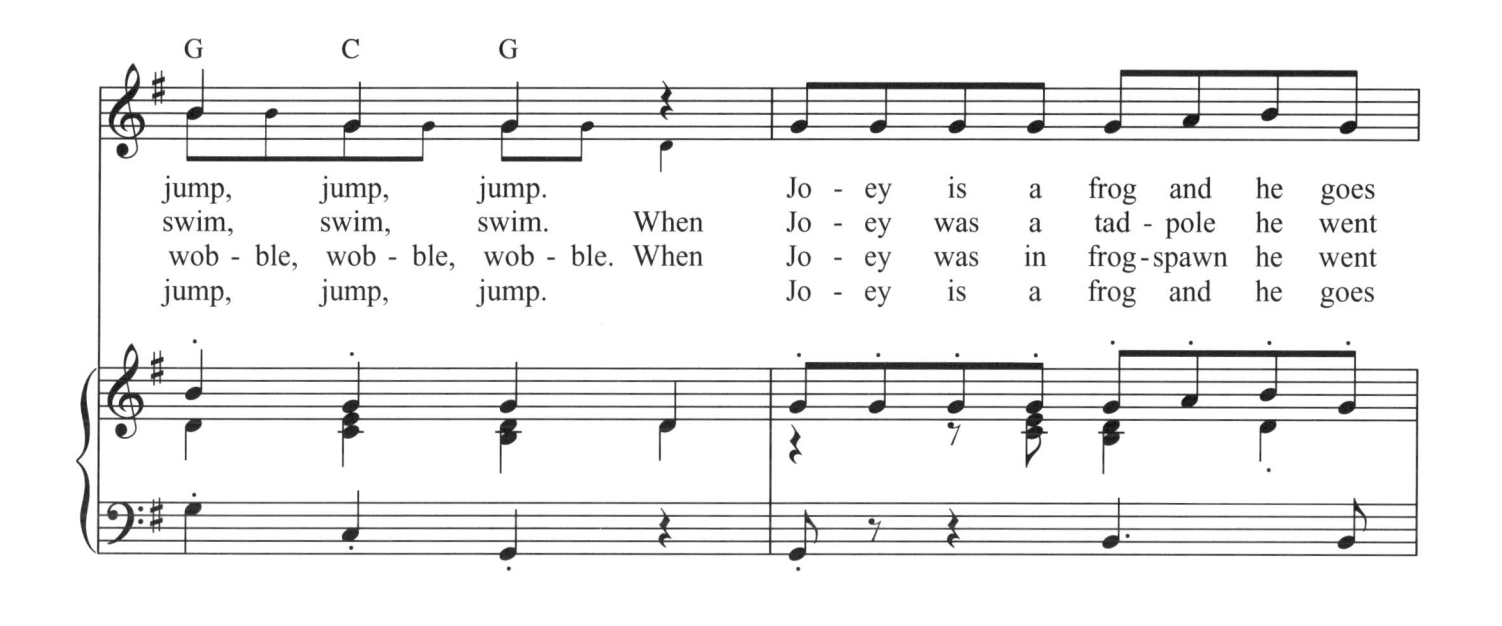

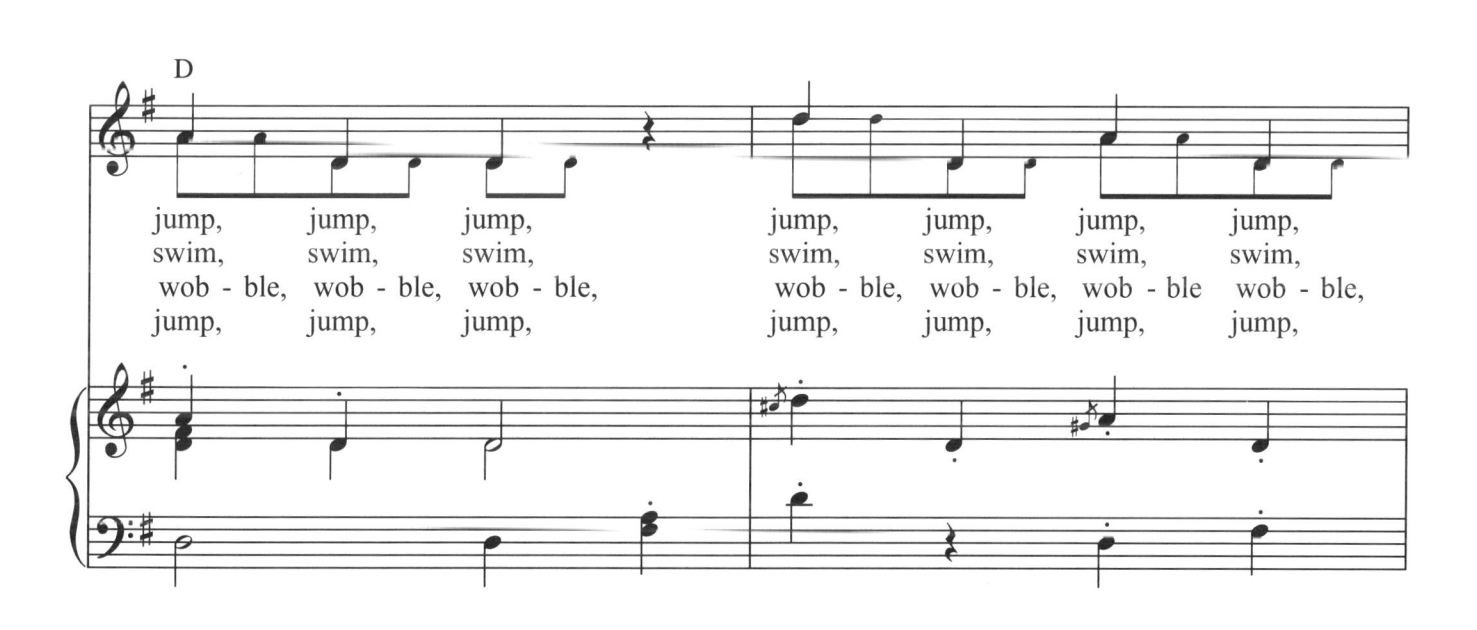

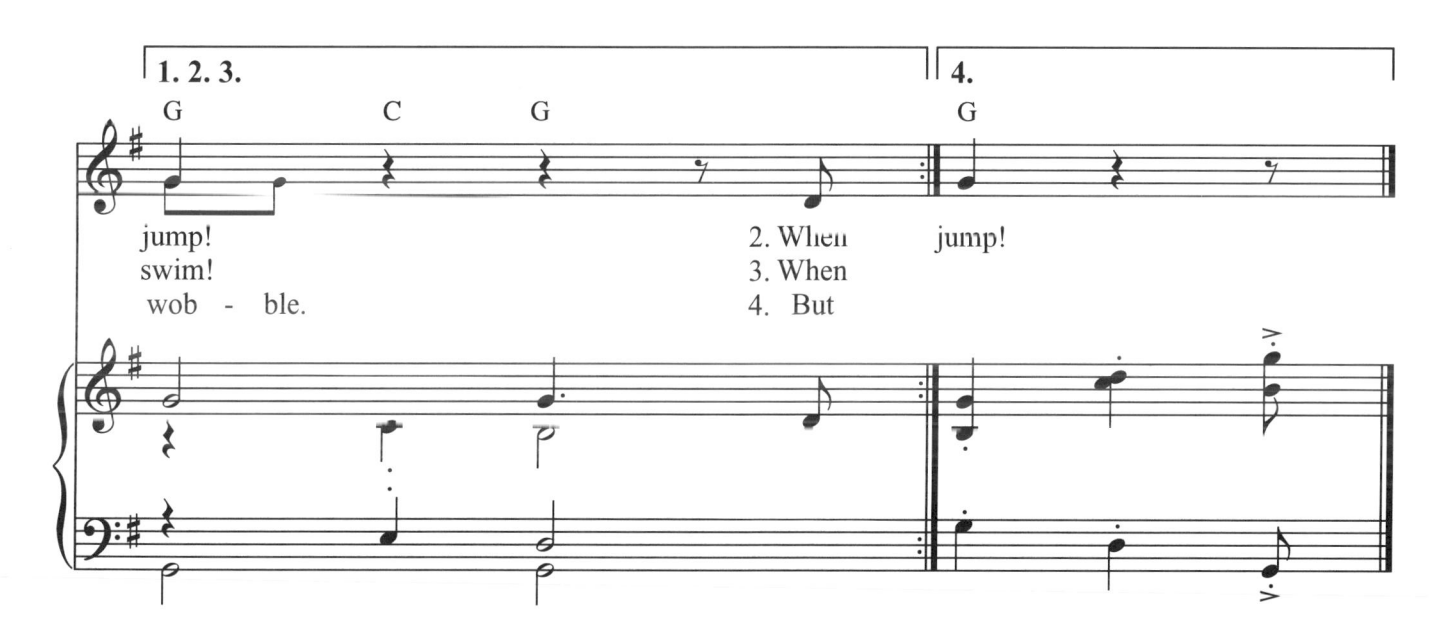

jump, jump, jump. Jo-ey is a frog and he goes
swim, swim, swim. When Jo-ey was a tad-pole he went
wob-ble, wob-ble, wob-ble. When Jo-ey was in frog-spawn he went
jump, jump, jump. Jo-ey is a frog and he goes

jump, jump, jump, jump, jump, jump, jump,
swim, swim, swim, swim, swim, swim, swim,
wob-ble, wob-ble, wob-ble, wob-ble, wob-ble, wob-ble wob-ble,
jump, jump, jump, jump, jump, jump, jump,

1. 2. 3.
jump!
swim!
wob-ble.

4.
2. When jump!
3. When
4. But

23

Follow The Silver Trail

Words and Music by
Niki Davies

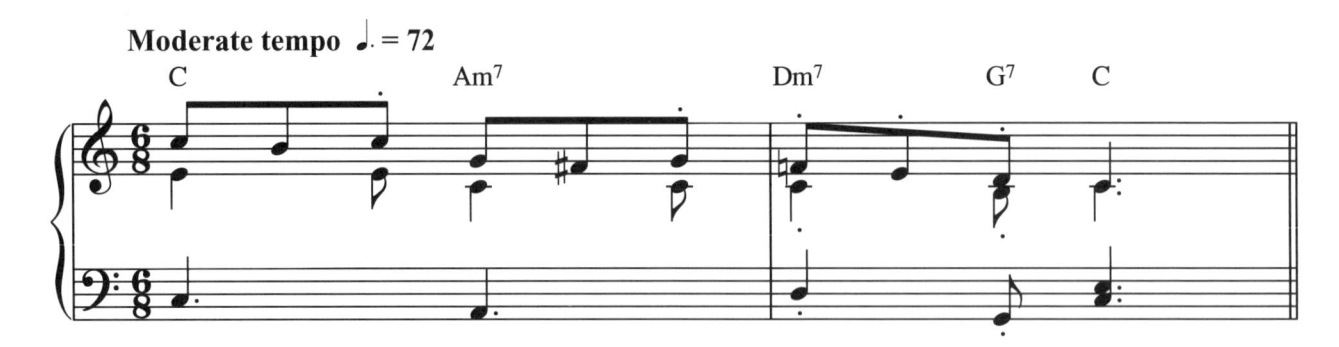

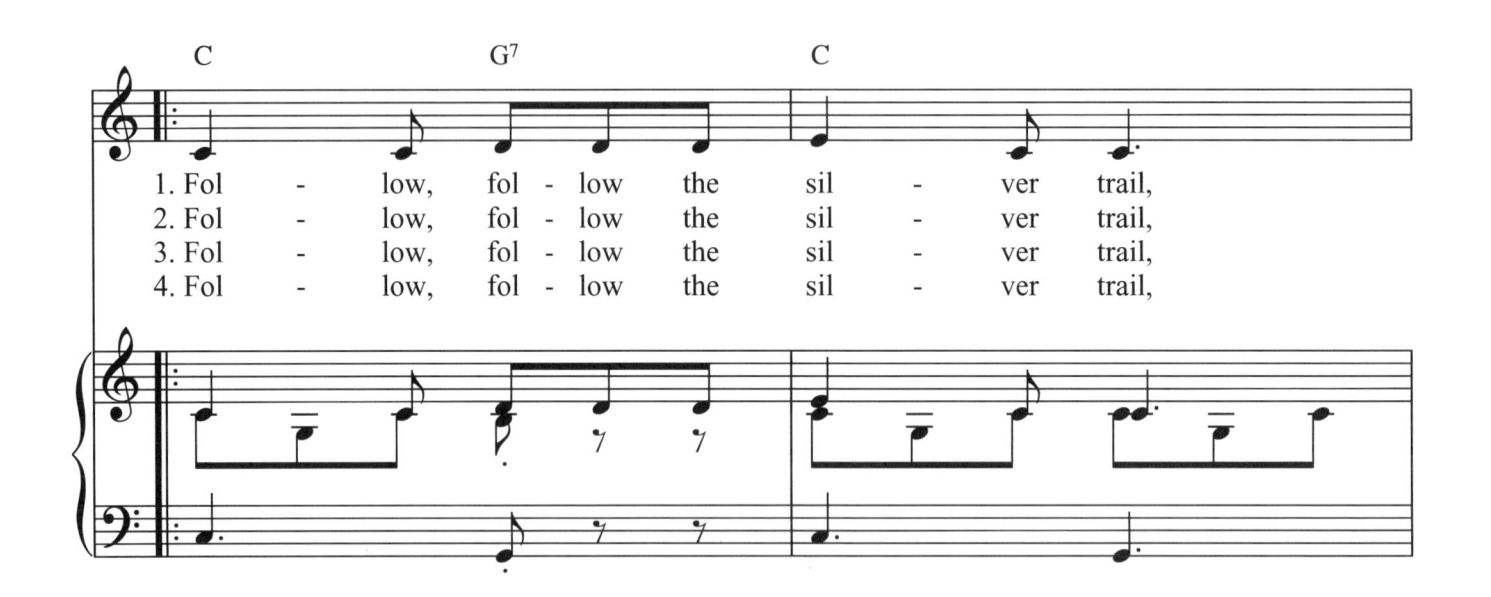

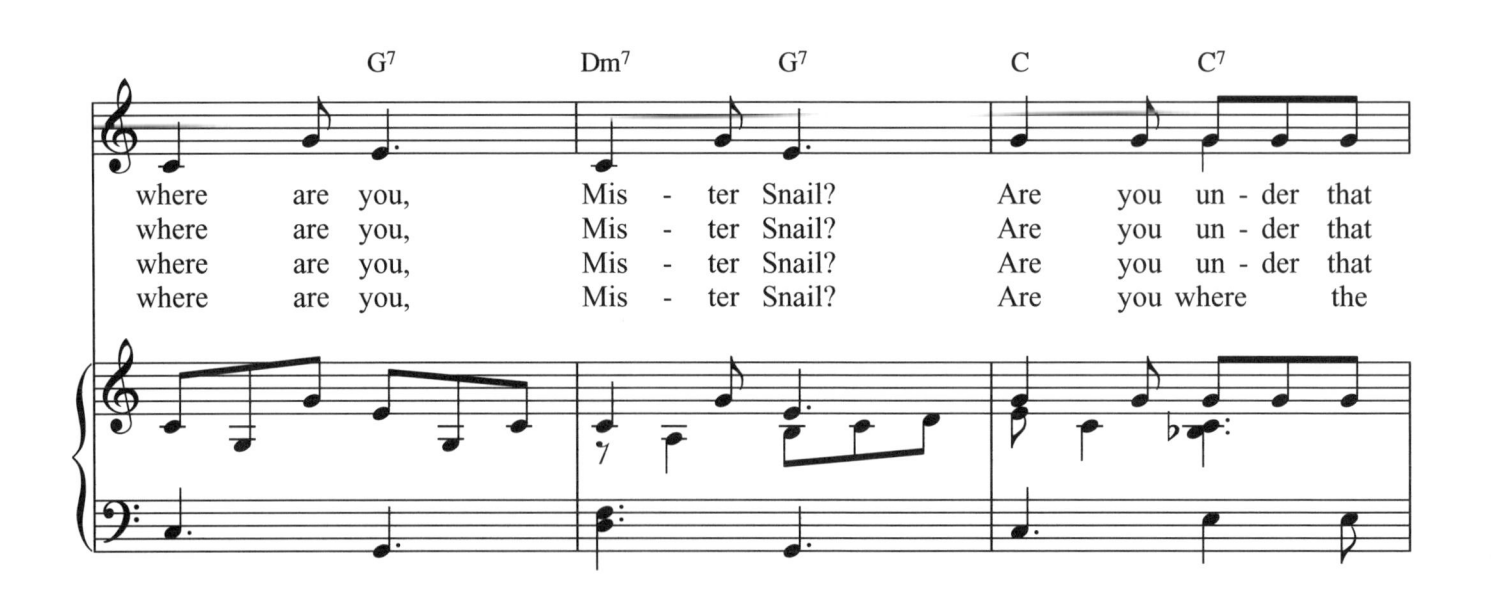

Moderate tempo ♩. = 72

1. Fol - low, fol - low the sil - ver trail, where are you, Mis - ter Snail? Are you un - der that
2. Fol - low, fol - low the sil - ver trail, where are you, Mis - ter Snail? Are you un - der that
3. Fol - low, fol - low the sil - ver trail, where are you, Mis - ter Snail? Are you un - der that
4. Fol - low, fol - low the sil - ver trail, where are you, Mis - ter Snail? Are you where the

© 2006 Out of the Ark Music, Surrey KT12 4RQ

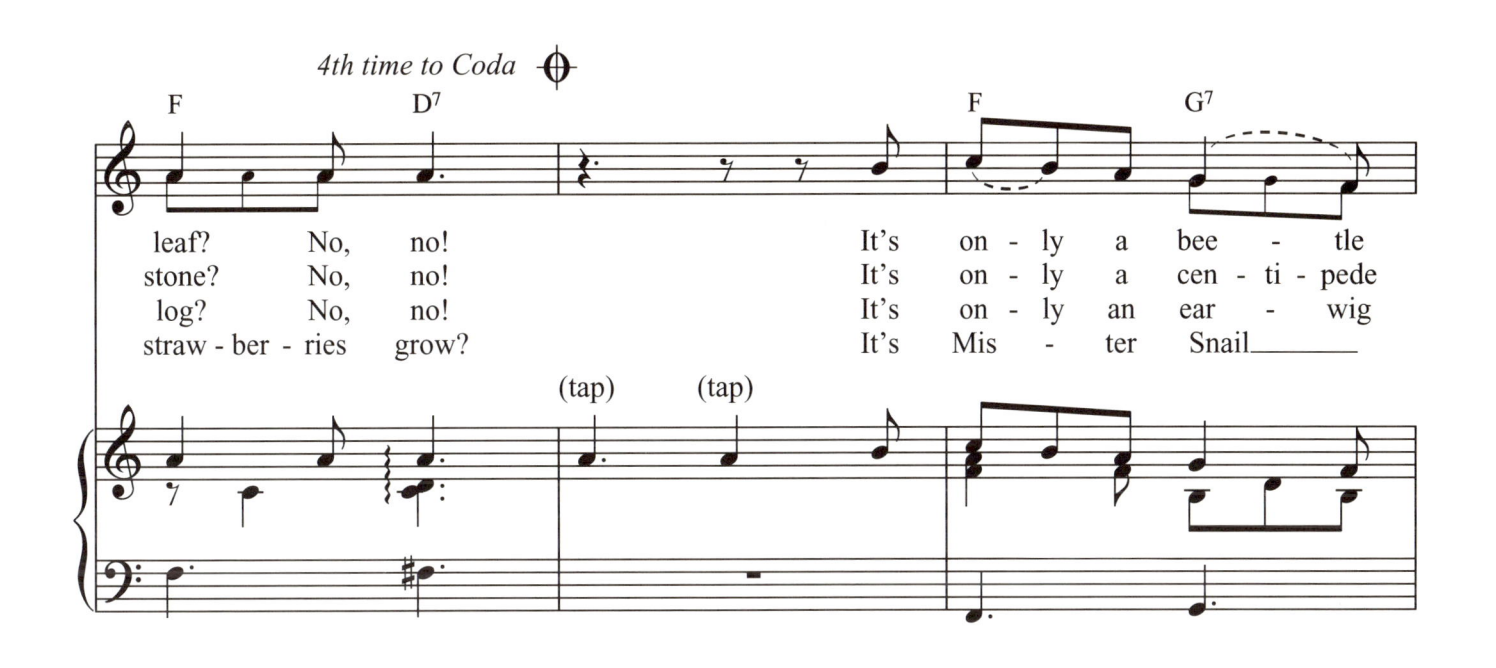

leaf? No, no! It's on-ly a bee - tle
stone? No, no! It's on-ly a cen - ti - pede
log? No, no! It's on-ly an ear - wig
straw-ber-ries grow? It's Mis - ter Snail

say - ing "Hel - lo".
say - ing "Hel - lo".
say - ing "Hel - lo".
say - ing "Hel - lo"!

CODA

poco rit.

Yes it's Mis - ter Snail say - ing "Hel - lo"!

Hey, Mister Bee

Words and Music by
Mark and Helen Johnson

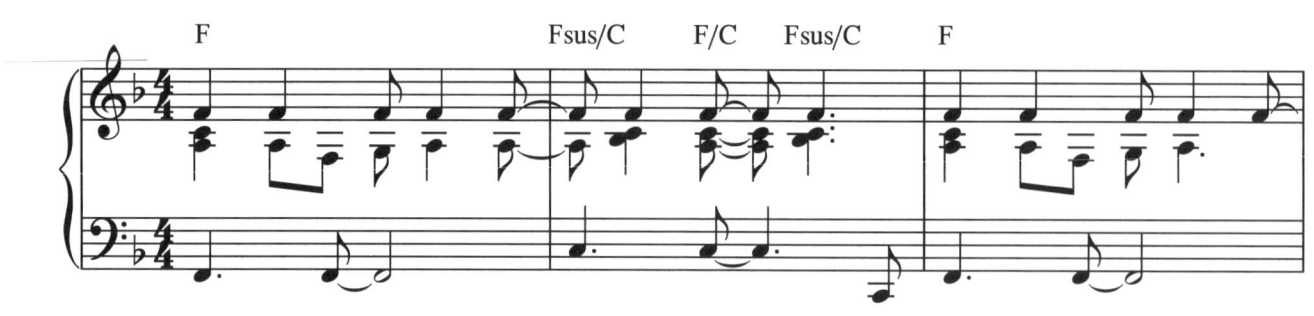

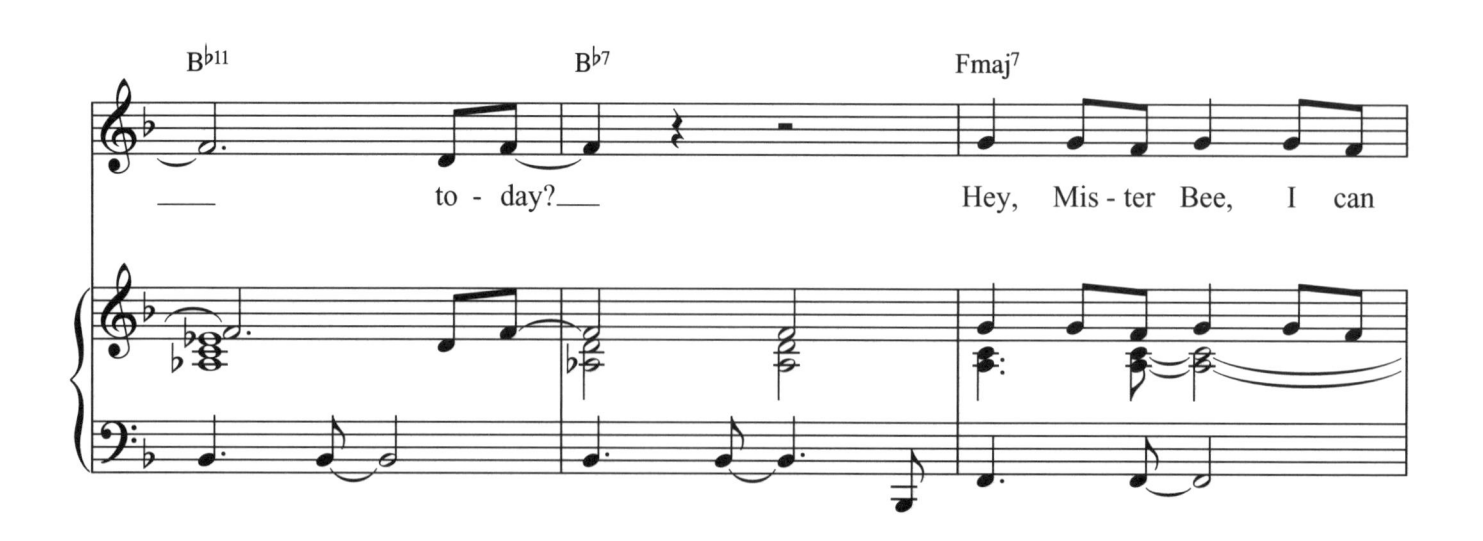

Gentle swing tempo ♩ = 116

Hey, Mis-ter Bee, can you see all the flow-ers a-round to-day? Hey, Mis-ter Bee, I can

© 2006 Out of the Ark Music, Surrey KT12 4RQ

see there are lots to be found___ to - day.__

When you've cho-sen a place,___ go dance in a fig-ure of eight__ to show ev-ery-one where to come for the pol-len to - day.__

1. 2.

27

3.
F
Gm7
to show ev - ery - one where to
Gm7/C
F
come for the pol - len to - day.
Gm7
So tell ev - ery - one we'll have
Gm7/C
poco rit.
F9
fun mak - ing ho - ney to - day!
(straight quavers)

Squirm

Words and Music by
Ann Beresford

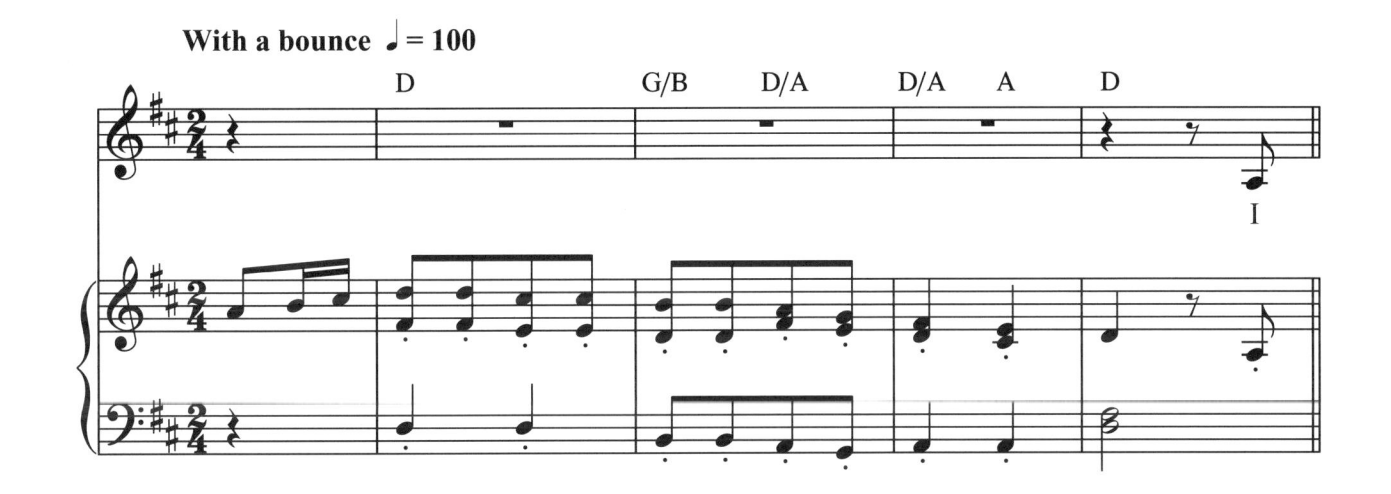

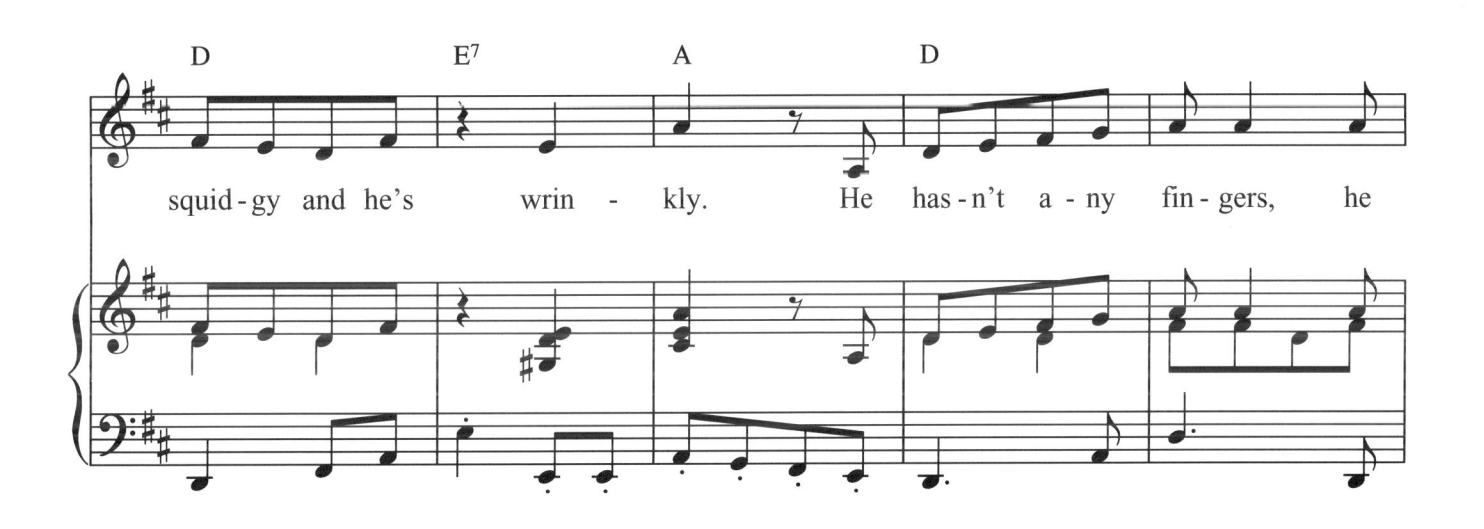

With a bounce ♩ = 100

I have a little friend who's not a bit like me, he's long and thin and squid-gy and he's wrin-kly. He has-n't a-ny fin-gers, he

© 2006 Out of the Ark Music, Surrey KT12 4RQ

hasn't any toes, I don't think he's got any eyes or mouth or nose. He hasn't got a front and he hasn't got a back, he hasn't any teeth to go snap, snap, snap! He doesn't make a buzzy noise, or even just a cheep, but he's

Asus4 A7 D A7sus4 D
ve - ry good at mak - ing earth down in the com - post heap.
Asus4 A7 D A7
1. D 2. D
I Have you
a little slower D/F♯ G poco rit. D
guessed who my friend is yet? I think I'll call him "Squirm". Cause he
A/D G/B D/A Em/G D/A A D
wrig - gles and he squig - gles through the ground. He's a worm.

We're Strong Ants

Words and Music by
Niki Davies

Bright & strong ♩ = 130

1. We're strong ants,
(2.) buzz-ing bees,
(3.) but-ter-flies,

strong ants, we carry the food as we march a-long. We're
buzz-ing bees, we're mak-ing ho-ney all day long. We're
but-ter-flies, we car-ry pol-len from flower to flower. We're

strong ants, strong ants, Hup, two three, four, strong ants.
buzz-ing bees, buzz-ing bees, buzz, buzz, buzz, buzz, buzz-ing bees.
but-ter-flies, but-ter-flies, flit-ter, flut-ter, but-ter-flies.

© 2006 Out of the Ark Music, Surrey KT12 4RQ

33

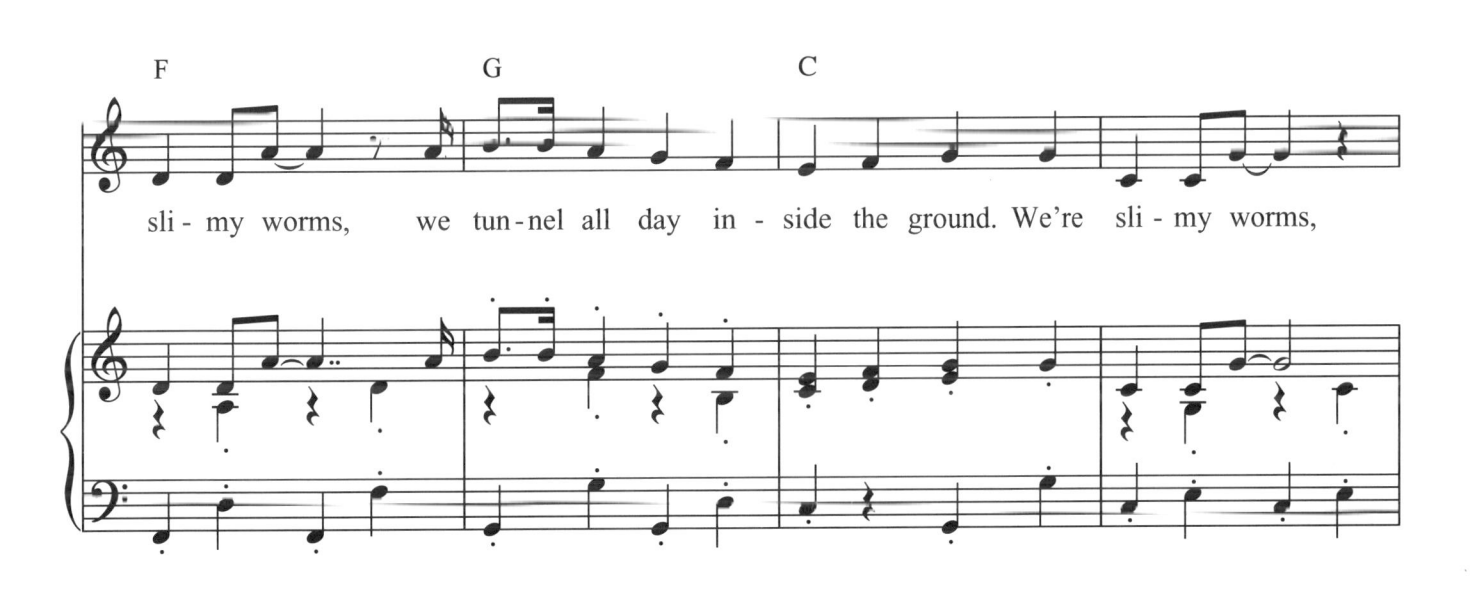

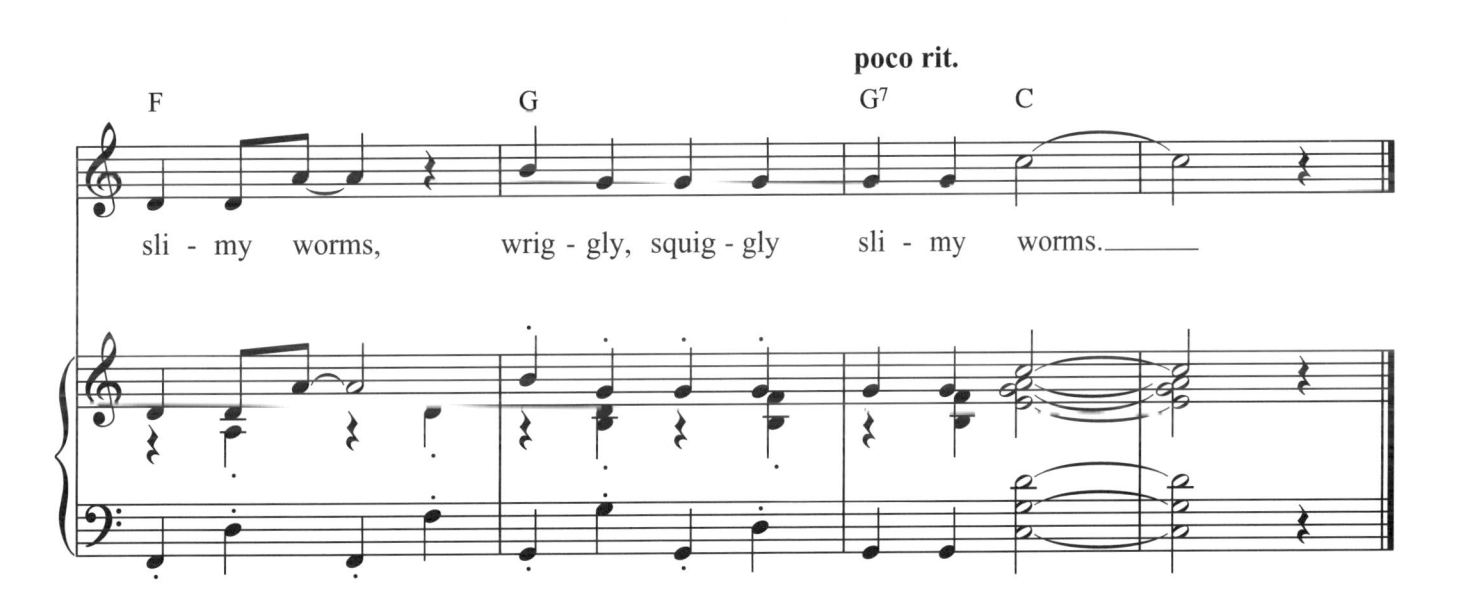

Pitter Patter Caterpillar

Words and Music by
Sha Armstrong

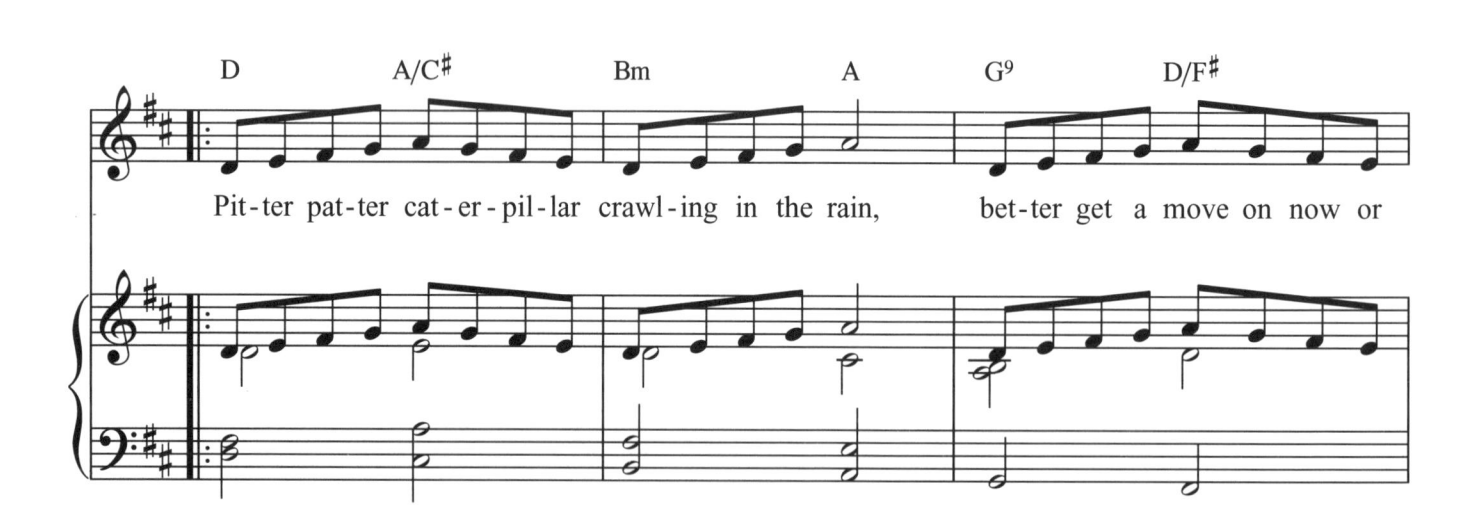

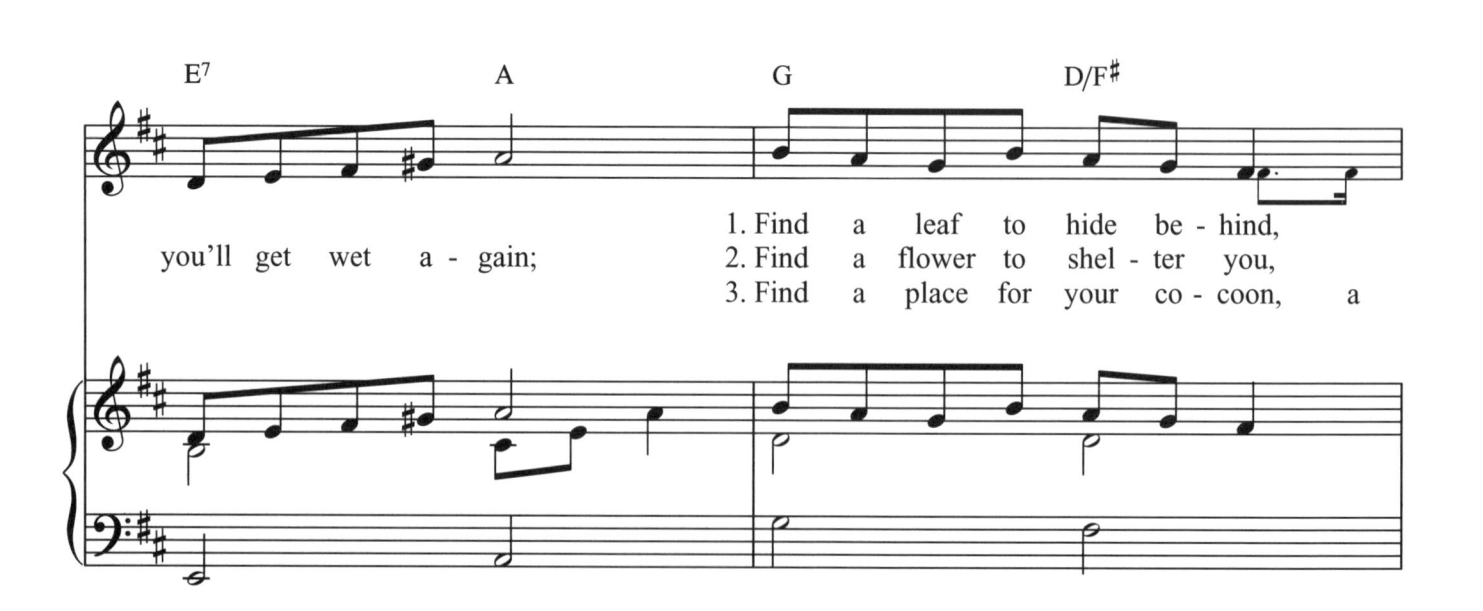

Unhurried ♩ = 90

Pit-ter pat-ter cat-er-pil-lar crawl-ing in the rain, bet-ter get a move on now or you'll get wet a-gain;

1. Find a leaf to hide be-hind,
2. Find a flower to shel-ter you,
3. Find a place for your co-coon, a

© 2006 Out of the Ark Music, Surrey KT12 4RQ

take a bite and you'll be fine.
take a rest, you'll feel brand new.
but-ter-fly you will be soon.
Pit-ter pat-ter cat-er-pil-lar crawl-ing in the

1. 2.
rain.

3.
rain. Crawl-ing in the rain.

Please Don't Squish Me!

Words and Music by
Mark and Helen Johnson

Gently, with movement ♩ = 96

You may think that I'm sca-ry, or say I'm on-ly small. Per-haps you think that I'm no good for a-ny-thing at all. But ac-tual-ly it's cle-ver, how I've been put to-geth-er, and if you get to know me you'll dis-co-ver that I'm cool! So

© 2006 Out of the Ark Music, Surrey KT12 4RQ

slightly faster
F/A B♭ C/E F B♭ F/A Gm
please don't squish me, please don't squash me! Put me back ex - act - ly
To Coda
C F F/A B♭ C♯dim B♭/D
where you got me. Please don't poke me, please don't prod me!
1. 2. D.𝄋 al Coda
CODA
B♭ F/A Gm C7 B♭/F F C7 B♭/F F
Let me be a hap-py mi - ni - beast. mi - ni - beast.
B♭ F/A Gm
Let me be a hap-py
poco rit.
C7 B♭/F F B♭ F/A Gm C7 B♭/F F
mi - ni - beast. Let me be a hap-py mi - ni - beast.

Out In The Garden

Words and Music by
Ann Beresford

Light 'n' bright ♩ = 120

1. Out in the gar-den   un-der-neath the stones,   you'll find mi-ni-beasts who don't have bones;
2. Out in the gar-den, round the flo-wer-pots,   you'll find mi-ni-beasts with stripes or spots,
3. Out in the gar-den, un-der-neath a pail,   you'll find mi-ni-beasts like slugs and snails,
4. Out in the gar-den, rest-ing on the leaves,   you'll find mi-ni-beasts like wasps and bees,
5. Out in the gar-den, by the com-post heap,   you'll find mi-ni-beasts that jump and leap,

© 2006 Out of the Ark Music, Surrey KT12 4RQ

earth - worms and wood lice, cen - ti - pedes and ants,
cat - er - pil - lars, spi - ders, la - dy - birds and ants,
bee - tles and ear - wigs, mil - li - pedes and ants,
but - ter - flies and green - flies, dra - gon - flies and ants,
cric - kets and spit bugs, grass - hop - pers and ants,

don't go sit - ting down on them you'll get them in your pants!

Spider Spins

Words and Music by
Niki Davies

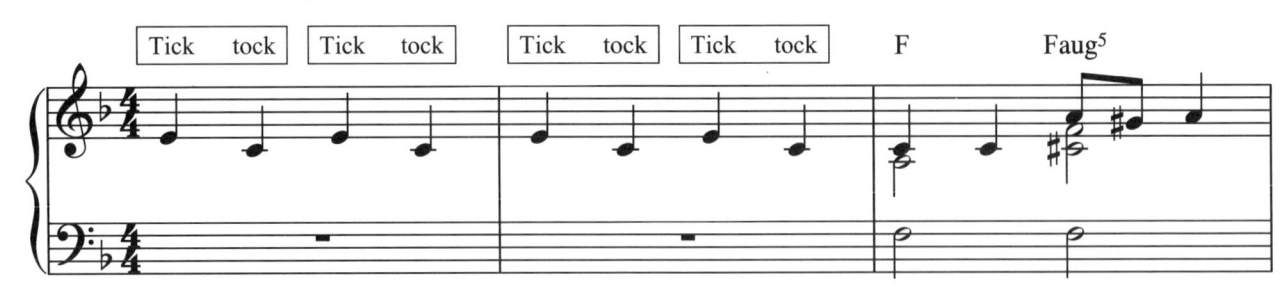

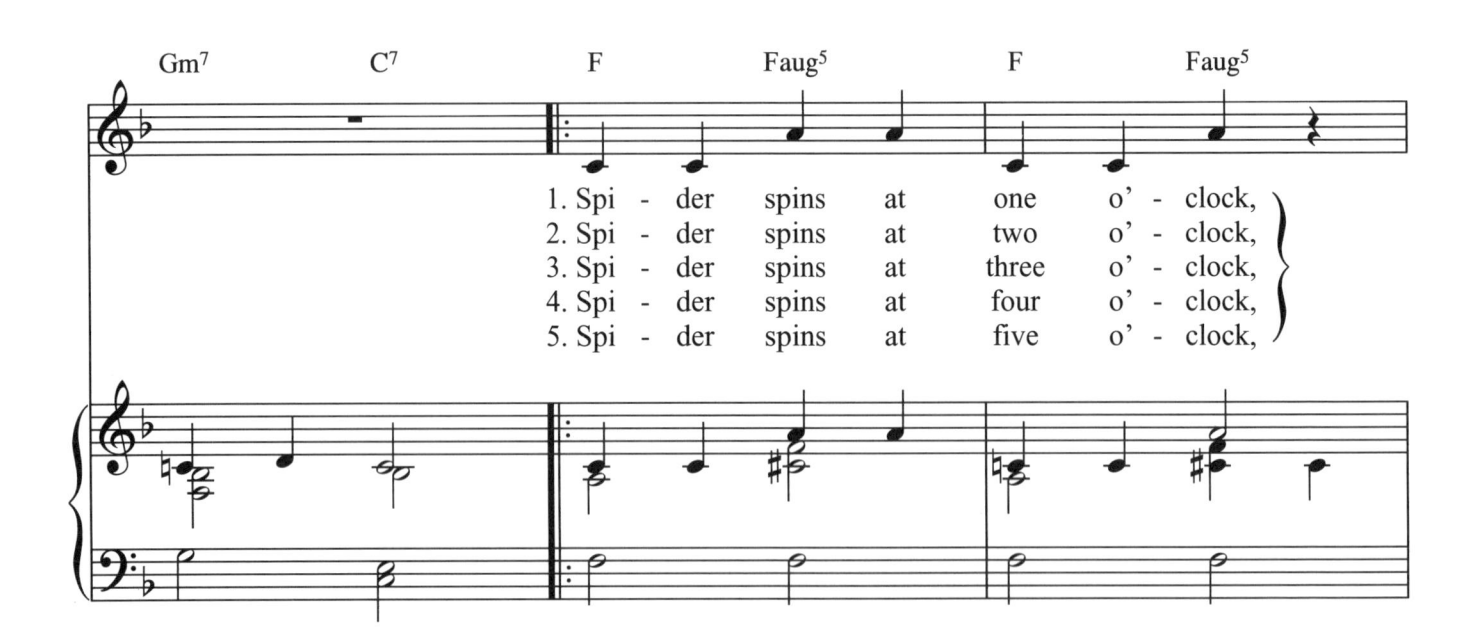

Moderate tempo ♩ = 104

Tick tock Tick tock Tick tock Tick tock F Faug5

Gm7 C7 F Faug5 F Faug5

1. Spi - der spins at one o'- clock,
2. Spi - der spins at two o'- clock,
3. Spi - der spins at three o'- clock,
4. Spi - der spins at four o'- clock,
5. Spi - der spins at five o'- clock,

Gm7 Cm7 C7 Gm7 C7

bu - sy, bu - sy legs, she does - n't stop;

© 2006 Out of the Ark Music, Surrey KT12 4RQ

spin - ning, spin - ning sil - ver threads,

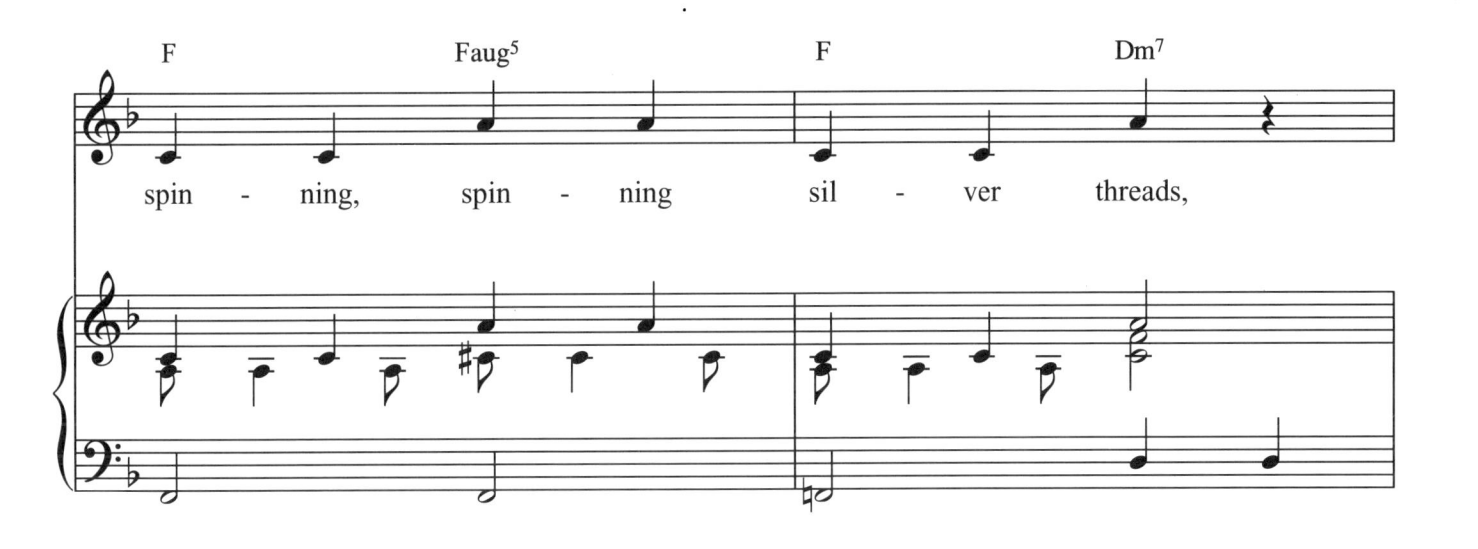

1 – 4.
bu - sy, bu - sy spi - der, make your web.

5.
bu - sy, bu - sy spi - der, make your web.

A B-U-G

Words and Music by
Sha Armstrong

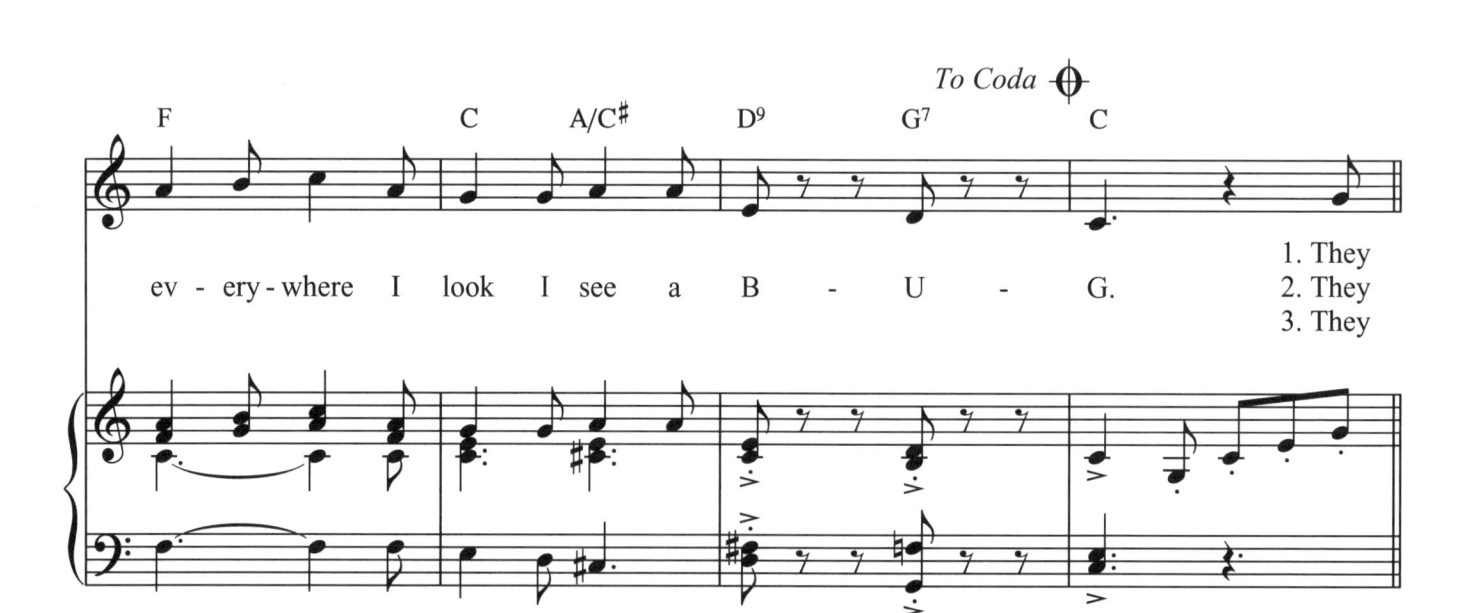

Bright ♩. = 90

A B-U-G, a B-U-G, everywhere I look I see a B-U-G.

1. They
2. They
3. They

© 2006 Out of the Ark Music, Surrey KT12 4RQ

43

Five Bluebottles

Traditional
Adapted by Mark and Helen Johnson

Medium swing feel ♩ = 110

1. Five
2. Four
3. Three
4. Two
5. One

blue-bot-tle(s) sit-ting on the wall,

five / four / three / two / one blue-bot-tle(s) sit-ting on the wall, and if one blue-bot-tle should ac-ci-den-tally fall___ Buzz!

Repeat 4 times

Last time: There'll be no blue-bot-tles, sit-ting on the wall.

© 2006 Out of the Ark Music, Surrey KT12 4RQ